Take up
Squash

Take up Sport

Titles in this series currently available or shortly to be published:

Take up Squash

Principal contributor:
Barry Mason
SRA Area and National Squad Coach
and International Referee

SPRINGFIELD BOOKS LIMITED

ISBN 0 947655 72 7

First published 1990 by
Springfield Books Limited
Springfield House, Norman Road, Denby Dale, Huddersfield
HD8 8TH

Edited, designed and produced by
White Line Press
60 Bradford Road, Stanningley, Leeds LS28 6EF

Editors: Noel Whittall and Philip Gardner
Design: Krystyna Hewitt
Diagrams: Chris Oxlade

Printed and bound in Great Britain

Photographic credits
Cover photograph: Action Plus
ICI Chemicals & Polymers Ltd: page 9
Stephen Line: pages 6, 8, 12, 15, 17, 20, 25, 30, 31, 58, 59,
    60.
All other photographs by Gordon Bellman Photography Ltd

Acknowledgements
Our thanks to Jon Gallacher and Clare Bulford, the Devon
junior players featured in the instructional photographs; and to
Wilson Sporting Goods for providing their equipment.

Contents

Introduction

Squash is one of the fastest growing participant sports of recent years. Only a few decades ago it belonged to the privileged few — pupils at private schools, university students and officers in the armed forces. Now there are more than 15 million players in over 100 countries worldwide. The game's availability has increased in line with its popularity; in Britain alone there are over 3 million players and 10,000 courts.

This immense popularity of squash stems largely from its simplicity — if you can hit a small rubber ball against a wall with a racket, you can play squash. There are no complicated techniques to be mastered before you begin to get enjoyment from playing.

Squash is also terrific exercise: you only need thirty or forty minutes on court regularly to feel the benefit. This makes it an activity which is ideally suited to the modern lifestyle, as a worthwhile game can be fitted into the lunchtime break or the journey home from work. Of course, if you really get hooked, it can also form the basis of a very enjoyable social life.

In the United Kingdom, the game has received an extra boost as many local authorities have provided leisure centres. These usually incorporate squash courts and help to make the game widely available. As well as regular coaching and competitions, junior sections and ladies' mornings are the rule rather than the exception at most centres and clubs.

Squash is a game which is played and enjoyed by both sexes. Wherever we have used "he", "him" or "his" in this book, it is intended to apply equally to both women and men.

> *Take up Squash* will help first-timers to get a good start in the game; it should also help enthusiasts who have been playing for some time but do not seem to be making progress. This "performance plateau" is often the result of simple errors in strokes or tactics which are highlighted in later chapters.

The history of the game

Until recently, squash was always referred to by its full name of *squash rackets*. This reflected its connection with the older game of *rackets* (or *racquets*), which was originally played in courtyards, and dates back at least five hundred years. Rackets is still played in a few places; both the court and the rackets themselves are larger than those for squash, and the ball is much harder and faster.

Squash is believed to have started at Harrow School around 1850, when some boys became tired of waiting for their chance to use the rackets court and played impromptu games in a much smaller confined area nearby. It soon became obvious that a ball with much less bounce was needed in this tighter space, and so one that could be readily *squashed* was used.

The successful spread of the game throughout the world was greatly helped by the British military forces, which built squash courts at most of their bases, both at home and overseas. Many of today's stars come from parts of the old Empire.

1

Above: *Jahangir Kahn and Jansher Kahn — world stars from Pakistan*

Right: *Transparent courts have brought squash to mass audiences.*

Squash and spectators

Because squash is played in a box-like room, there are obvious problems when it comes to letting lots of spectators view the action. This has been tackled by using glass and Perspex extensively for the walls, and the finals of major events are now usually staged on see-through courts.

The first glass-backed championship court appeared at Abbeydale Park, Sheffield, in 1971, and about four hundred spectators witnessed the final of the British Open. Now a crowd of over 3,000 can sit in comfort in the Wembley Conference Centre and see the same event, thanks to the advances in transparent court construction.

2

For many years attempts to show play on television were not very successful because the dull-coloured, fast-moving ball was frequently invisible through the cameras. However, recent technological progress has developed a reflective squash ball, which means that television viewers can now clearly follow the pattern of a rally. There have already been many "booms" in the sport since it was first played, but the greatest will surely come if the game makes a breakthrough on television world-wide.

If this book manages to awaken an interest in the game for you, you could just be part of the biggest boom yet — good squashing!

The aim of the game

Squash is a game for two people. The object is very simple: you just have to hit a small ball and make it rebound from a wall in such a way that your opponent cannot play a fair return. We deal with what is fair in Chapter 4.

2

Equipment and clothing

The only special items of equipment required for squash are a racket and a ball. At most public courts you will be able to hire a racket for a small sum. You will probably have to buy a squash ball, but these are not expensive.

Rackets

As soon as you have developed a taste for the game, you will want your own racket: the range is very wide, but you should not buy one of the expensive ones until you have gained some experience. The racket frames are now usually made from graphite composites, and the strings from man-made fibres, although gut is still preferred by some top-grade players.

There is a wide range of materials available for the grip on the handle, and you will soon find one which suits you.

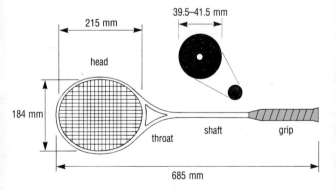

Figure 1 The racket and ball must conform to the standard dimensions.

Squash balls

The ball is a small hollow rubber sphere. It will be marked with a coloured spot which tells you what its speed is. A fast ball bounces further than a slow one. As a newcomer to the game, you will find it easiest to play with a fast ball, as the higher bounce gives you more time to reach it. The colour codes for the spots are:

Yellow: super-slow
White: slow
Red: medium
Blue: fast

As you hit the ball around the court, it will warm up. This raises the pressure of the gas inside it and makes it behave in a more lively manner. Squash players always "knock up" for five minutes before a game: this gets the ball up to working temperature as well as loosening up the players!

Warming the ball can be a problem for youngsters and raw beginners who have not the power or skill to hit it hard. If this is the case, try scrubbing the ball against the floor a few times with your foot before playing.

Occasionally, a ball will burst during a game. When this happens, the players bring its replacement up to match speed during a brief knock-up before scoring re-starts.

Clothing

Your clothing should be lightweight, simple and comfortable. A T-shirt is ideal, worn with shorts or a skirt. As your opponent will have difficulty sighting the ball against dark clothing, keep to white or pale colours.

Footwear

White socks are usual. Squash calls for lots of sudden acceleration and rapid changes in direction, so well-fitting socks are important. As you will get hot, your socks must be absorbent: the cotton type with a looped pile are particularly comfortable.

Most of the better sports-shoe manufacturers produce special squash shoes, but you will be able to start playing by using ordinary trainers or tennis shoes. Don't just walk onto the court in the trainers you wear on the street, though — grit and dirt from outside must not be transferred onto the floor. Another essential is that your shoes must *not* have black soles: these quickly mark the floor, and as this is a particularly costly part of the court, you will win no friends by leaving unsightly traces of your chases after the elusive ball.

Spectacles

There is always the risk of being accidentally hit by your opponent's racket, so if you wear glasses when you play, make sure that they have lenses made from safety glass or plastic.

3

4

On-court clothing for men and women should be light, simple and functional. Michelle Martin's outfit is particularly attractive.

3

The court

The standard squash court is basically a rectangular room, 32 ft long by 21 ft wide (9.75 m x 6.40 m), with white walls and a wooden floor. Sometimes the rear wall is made of glass or clear plastic, so that spectators can watch the game. Some prestige events, such as the British Open Championship, are played on an all-Perspex court, which enables a much wider audience to see the action.

Although the court is not very large, you will be amazed how much energy can be expended in it in a very short time!

The walls

You enter the court through a door which fits flush with the back wall. Facing you, on the front wall, there are three horizontal red lines. From the ground upwards, these are the *board*, the *cut line* and the *boundary line* (often also called the *out-of-court line*).

The area below the board is called the *tin*; it is usually covered in sheet metal or thin plywood, so that the ball makes a distinctive sound when it hits it. The tin is really the equivalent of the net in tennis, with the board taking the place of the white tape at the top of the net.

The *cut line* is six feet (1.8 m) from the ground. It is only important during service, when the ball must strike the wall above it.

The *boundary line* on the front wall is fifteen feet (4.6 m) from the ground.

The side walls each have just one line. These are continuations of the boundary line, and slope down to meet the back wall seven feet (2.1 m) from the ground. The boundary line continues horizontally across the back wall.

During play, the ball must hit the wall below the boundary line if it is to remain *in court*.

In a court which has been used for any time, there will be "skid marks" towards the rear of the side walls where the heads of rackets have made contact. You will learn the significance of these later.

No height is specified for the ceiling of the court, but naturally it must be substantially higher than the boundary line.

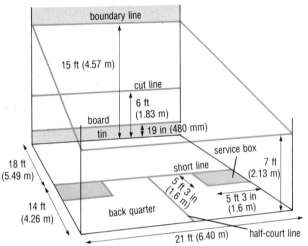

Figure 2 The markings and dimensions of the court

Court sense and safety
Treat the door onto the court with care:

● *Always* check that the door handle has dropped into its recess before starting play.

● *Never* open the door from outside without checking that it is safe to do so. If the door does not have a spy-hole, then knock, and wait for the players inside to open it.

The floor

The floor of a good-quality court is normally made out of maple, and is slightly sprung. The markings on it are simple:

A red line crosses the court 18 ft (5.5 m) from the front wall. This is the *short line*, and the one at right angles to it is the *half-court line*, which connects the centre of the short line to the back wall.

The large rectangles which these lines form at the rear of the court are called the *back quarters*.

At each end of the short line, a box is marked. These are the *service boxes*.

Like the cut line, all the lines on the floor are of significance only during service — once a rally is under way, they are ignored.

In squash, unlike tennis, a ball which touches a line is *out*. Similarly, when serving, your foot must be right *in* the appropriate box — touching the line is not good enough.

5

The maple floor shows clearly on this shot of Simon Parke and Stacey Ross competing in an Under-16s Open Championship.

4

The game

In squash, the aim of each player is to play the ball before it bounces twice so that it does not go *down* or *out*. A ball that hits the board, the tin, or the floor on its way to the front wall is said to be *down*. It is *out* if it hits the boundary line or anything above that line. *Not up* describes a ball which is allowed to bounce twice on the floor; in squash, *not up* is not exactly the same as *down*. There is no restriction on the number of times the ball may contact the walls.

To ensure certain victory in a squash match now seems quite simple — you only have to remember not to hit the ball down or out, or to let it bounce twice. All this is rather easier said than done...

Serving and scoring

The players spin a racket to decide who is to serve first. The winner can choose which service box to serve from. To make the serve, the player must have at least one foot inside the service box. The ball is thrown into the air, and must then be struck so that it hits the front wall above the cut line before bouncing in the opponent's back quarter of the court.

As long as you keep the service, you serve from alternate boxes.

After hitting the front wall, the ball can hit any other wall on its way to bouncing in the opposite rear quarter. Figure 3 shows paths of the ball from the right-hand service box, all of which are legal. Note that it simply has to bounce in the opposite back quarter and not, as some novices imagine, in the opposite service box.

Watch your feet: don't risk losing the serve by failing to keep one foot *completely inside* the box.

Take care to make your serve a good one: since the rules were amended in 1989, you are allowed only one attempt. If you fail, the right to serve passes immediately to your opponent. Each time the service changes, the new server can choose which side to serve from.

At the start of each new game in a match, the winner of the previous game serves first.

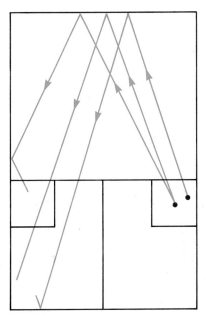

Figure 3 All of these serves are legal, provided that the server has at least one foot in the box and the ball hits the front wall above the cut line.

6

Under-23 competitors Samantha Langley and Cassie Jackman during an energetic rally

Rallies

Each session of play between serves is called a *rally*. Once the service has been made, the two players play alternate shots to the front wall between the board and the boundary line until one of them makes an error and hits the ball down, out or lets it bounce twice. Remember, you are allowed to bounce the ball off the back and side walls both before and after it hits the front wall.

If you win the rally after having served, you gain a *point*; if you win the rally when receiving, you gain the right to serve.

Game

A game is made up of a series of rallies. The first player to score nine points wins the game. If the score reaches eight-all, the receiver has the choice of deciding to play to nine points (call "no set!"), or to ten ("set two!"). This call can only be made at 8—8, and once made cannot be altered.

Unlike some other racket games, you do not have to be two points clear to win a game. So if you overhear someone gasping out the score 19–18 you can tell them that they should have had a rest a long time ago!

Match

A match usually consists of the best of five games, so the winner is the first player to win three games. A match can take as little as ten minutes or longer than two hours!

Use standard scoring!
Although the the nine-point game described in this book is the only official international version of squash, you may sometimes hear of different scoring rules being used — for example, where a point is scored at the end of each rally, regardless of who served, and the first player to 15 points wins the game.

These variations can appear attractive, but once you have developed an appreciation of the different skills involved in attack and defence, you will realise that they can also change the nature of the game. Learn to play and enjoy the genuine article!

5

Basic skills

Many players learn their squash without any formal guidance. This makes it easy to develop bad habits which are hard to get rid of. If you are a complete beginner, this chapter should help you to avoid such habits.

You will soon become an effective competitor at squash if you can master four basics early on:

 grip
● swing
● movement
● balance

Grip

Control of the racket head is difficult without the correct grip.

7

8

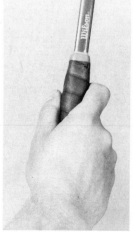

The grip — note how the "V" between thumb and forefinger points down the leading edge of the shaft, and the first two fingers are spread slightly.

In photos 7 and 8, see how the the "V" between thumb and forefinger points along the leading edge of the shaft: the first two fingers should be spread slightly as shown.

You can play both forehand and backhand strokes with the same grip — indeed, the game is often so fast that there is little time to make adjustments from one side to the other.

9

There is an exception to every rule! Peter Marshall is surely unique in using this double-handed grip for both backhand and forehand shots.

The squash swing

The fundamental skill needed in squash is the ability to hit the ball accurately, parallel to the side walls of the court. For safety reasons, you cannot swing at a squash ball as freely as in, say, tennis. This is because in squash the opponents are both on the same side of the "net", so you must develop a racket swing which is compact, not an uncontrolled swipe.

Attention to three main points will help you develop the right style of swing:

● Stand sideways-on to the front wall

● Keep the wrist of your racket hand "cocked", so that the racket head is slightly higher than the wrist

● Follow-through

It is most natural to swing the racket *across* your body, for both forehand and backhand strokes, so it is essential to be *sideways-on* to the front wall. Because the front wall is the primary target, it is easy for a beginner to make the mistake of standing square-on to it. This is a particularly common problem among self-taught players, so if you have been playing for a little time and your game has reached a performance plateau, this may well be the reason.

Cocking your wrist means that it is in its strongest position and so can keep the head of the racket firmly under control. It also saves time when the ball arrives, because the racket head will be slightly above your wrist at the moment of impact — the ideal position.

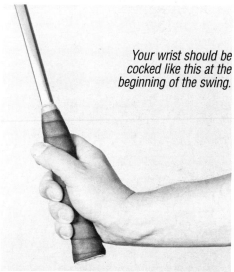

Your wrist should be cocked like this at the beginning of the swing.

10

The follow-through is straightforward: simply make sure that the racket head follows the intended path of the ball.

How to check your swing

- Stand with your back about eighteen inches (45 cm) from a wall

- Play a forehand stroke at an imaginary ball roughly a racket's length in front of your left knee

- Pause briefly at the end of your follow-through and then imagine that the ball is in front of your right knee and play a backhand stroke in the opposite direction.

If your racket is not in danger of hitting the wall at the end of either stroke, you have developed the correct compact style which the game demands.

Basic movement on court

Correct movement on court is another skill often over-looked in the early stages through a desire to "get on with the game".

As mentioned earlier, squash is to a great extent a *sideways* game, and by turning sideways *first* you can make a much more economical approach to the ball.

Figures 4 and 5 show this initial turn of the body which is the key to good movement.

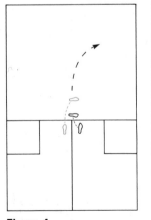 

Figure 4   **Figure 5**

Movement from the T to the front (Figure 4) and rear (Figure 5) forehand courts — turn first, then move.

You need space in which to approach the ball and to play it, and efficient movement enables you to make this space. As your game progresses, the use of space becomes more and more important, and we deal with it again in the section on tactics.

Balance

Balance is closely allied to movement. For good control and accuracy of shot it is essential to be well balanced as you strike. Try to arrive at the ball sideways-on, with your weight on the leading foot.

Putting it all together

There is a theory that we learn skills by one of three methods. Some of us read or listen to instructions and then carry them out; others watch and then imitate; a large number simply have a go and learn by trial and error. Whichever method suits you, do keep in mind that there is always something to learn: the most successful players are those who identify problems and reduce their errors to a minimum.

Initial practice on the court

Don't bother about scoring as soon as you get onto a squash court: try a co-operative rally with a partner, just hitting the ball backwards and forwards to each other via the front wall, as Jon and Clare are doing in photograph 11.

Change sides occasionally so that you have to play both forehand and backhand shots. Remember to try turning sideways to hit, and make sure there is space for your swing.

11

Jon and Clare playing a co-operative rally

6

Some common problems

The ball

As a beginner, you should make things as easy as possible for yourself by playing with a "fast" ball — that means one with a blue dot. Even so, you will probably find that it does not bounce as high as you expect: on some courts during a cold winter it will hardly bounce at all. You may be faced with a chicken-and-egg situation in which you need to warm the ball up by hitting it, but you are having difficulty hitting it because it is not warm enough! If that is the case, put some life into it by putting it under your foot and scrubbing it vigorously on the floor.

As your squash improves, try a slower ball (red or white dot). You will eventually graduate to the yellow-dot ball which is commonly used for competitive play.

Side walls

Other racket sports such as tennis and badminton do not have side walls, and it takes a little time to discover the effect these have. Beginners usually tend to chase a ball towards the side only to find it shooting back towards or even past them, and so having to make a hurried shot.

Try this simple exercise to get the feel of how the ball performs when it meets a side wall:

● Stand on one side of the court and gently lob the ball from your hand to strike the opposite side wall before landing on the floor: the ball will return to where you are standing (see Figure 6).

● Now repeat the operation, but try to make the ball land on the floor *before* it hits the opposite wall: you will have to walk across the court to retrieve it (see Figure 7).

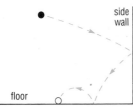
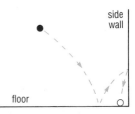

Figure 6 A ball which hits the wall before the floor will bounce back out into the court.

Figure 7 If the ball hits the floor before the wall, it will stay close to the wall.

12

No matter where it's coming from — keep your eye on the ball!

The lesson from this is to watch the ball carefully as it heads from the front wall towards a side wall. If you are confident that it will hit the wall first and the floor second, then you can wait for it to come towards you, thus creating *space* in which to operate. If you are sure that the ball will hit the floor first and then the wall, you can make your approach accordingly.

What about the doubtful ball? Remember that it is easier to move towards the ball than away from it — so if in doubt, hold back.

At first the side wall can seem like an enemy, but as your judgement improves it will become your ally.

The back corners

When you look around the court, you will almost certainly notice some areas of wear towards the rear of the side walls — the skid marks referred to at the end of Chapter 2. These marks on the wall will undoubtedly be a combination of black, green or blue rubber from squash balls, black streaks from graphite rackets, and a multitude of lines of varying hue and length caused by taped racket heads. There may even be chunks of plaster missing from the wall. All this is the result of players flailing at a ball which has lured them into a back corner.

These back corners are responsible for the demolition of a good number of rackets. You can avoid many of the back-corner problems by developing good movement patterns which get you to the corner before the ball.

Figure 8 illustrates typical good movement patterns. If you practise these approaches you will often save yourself embarrassment in the back corners — and perhaps the cost of a new racket.

There will inevitably be occasions when the ball arrives in the corner before you can, but if your movement is good you will be able to enlist the aid of the side wall by bouncing the ball off it with a stroke called a *boast* (see page 44).

Over-running

Watch a game of junior soccer and you will often observe a cluster of bodies surrounding a bobbing ball and a goalkeeper in isolation at each end of the pitch. Their keenness is such that most of the players are chasing the ball. It is this same understandable enthusiasm which is the downfall of many squash players — and not only beginners. You will naturally be so keen to return the ball that you will often find yourself setting off in a straight line towards what you judge to be its destination. The result will inevitably be a cramped stroke which will either fall into the "down, out or not-up" category, or be tactically poor and so give your opponent a distinct advantage. One of the hardest lessons for beginners to absorb is the need to anticipate where the next shot is going and to get to it *at just the right time*. Over-running is both exhausting and inefficient.

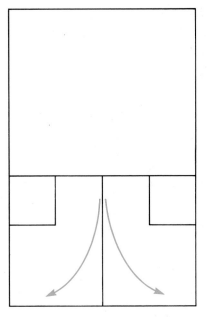

Figure 8 It is best to follow a path like this to move from the T to the back corners.

7

Tactics

Controlling the T

Early in your squash career you will meet the expression "controlling the T". This is the key to squash tactics, and can be the source of a certain sadistic delight as you dominate the centre of the court and watch your opponent repeatedly having difficulty in the back corners.

The T is the junction between the short line and the half-court line (see Figure 2 on page 14). When you made your initial tour of the court, you probably noticed that the markings on the floor showed signs of the heaviest wear at this point. This is because the T is the control point of the arena, and success in the battle campaign largely depends on whether or not you can spend more time there than your opponent.

The advantages of gaining control are immense:

- you can arrange for your opponent's journeys to the corners of the court to be longer than yours

- you can take the ball a little sooner than he does, so giving him less time for recovery

- you have longer to prepare yourself for your next stroke, and therefore can be much more devious.

Naturally, the longer you can keep this up, the more pleasurable it becomes! However, you will soon appreciate that you have no divine right to the T — it has to be earned by playing the right shots and moving quickly to take up the new position.

Obstruction and positioning

Newcomers to the game are constantly advised of the importance of the T and how they must return there after every shot, but coaches sometimes fail to add "provided it is safe to do so". The main dangers are being struck by a racket or the ball, or committing the offence of interference. Either way you lose the rally, but you might also get a nasty bruising.

Interference

The rules of the game state that a player should be free to play the ball to any part of the front wall. It is up to you not to obstruct your opponent in this, yet if you watch a game closely, at any level, you will see apparent infringements of this rule in almost every rally!

The easiest way to understand the law of interference is to picture a triangle formed by two imaginary lines drawn along the floor from the ball to the two front corners of the court and the bottom of the tin. If you are in that triangle (or even if your racket is) as your opponent is about to strike, then you are obviously infringing the rules and maybe stepping into danger.

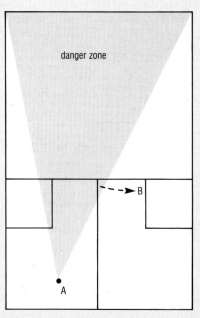

Figure 9 A, about to strike, must be given a fair chance of hitting the front wall, so B must move out of the "danger zone".

29

Even the stars can get into a tangle on the court. Rodney Martin plays around Jahangir Kahn during the 1989 British Open Championship.

Basic on-court tactics

Watch the ball

To have any chance of success at squash, you must keep your eye on the ball all the time so that you are constantly in a position to take advantage of the situation. By watching the ball you will see the difficulties your opponent is getting himself into, and should be able to anticipate his next shot so that the pressure can be maintained.

Play straight

You will often be told to "play straight" — which means parallel to the side walls. The compact swing which you have learned is designed to help in this, but you also need to understand *why* playing straight is so often a point-winning tactic.

14

This junior player is perfectly positioned for a straight drive, parallel to the side wall.

Let's look at players *A* and *B* playing a typical point: *A* is less experienced than *B*, but is in position on the T when *B* sends the ball to the front forehand quarter of the court. *A* moves forward from the T and decides to play deep to one of the back corners to retain his advantage of being in front of *B* (see Figure 10).

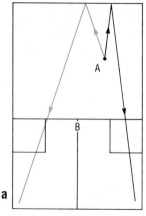

He thinks this is a good shot to play, because there appears to be much more room to *A*'s left; also, as *B* is right-handed, the ball will be going to *B*'s backhand corner. Down the right-hand wall there is not so much room, and also it is on *B*'s forehand side.

A rushes forward, facing the front wall, and instinctively drives the ball across the court in the direction of *B*'s backhand corner. This is exactly what most untutored squash players would do.

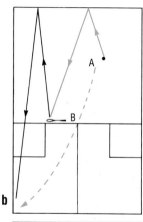

B, more experienced, turns sideways to face the left-hand wall and plays a controlled backhand straight down the wall to a good length (second bounce close to the back wall). He then steps aside to enjoy the fun as *A* scampers past him in pursuit of his next shot.

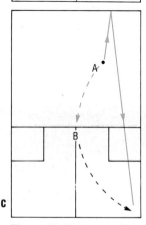

The moral is that in order to gain control of the command post, the T, it is much more effective to play *straight*. If *A* had done that in the first place, it would have been *B* who was floundering in the back corner and *A* who would have been back on the T (see Figure 10c).

Figure 10 Playing straight

When he has gained a little more experience, A will have developed the skill of automatically turning sideways, approaching the ball with the correct movement pattern and making space in which to play a straight forehand shot.

Cross-court shots

Of course, you cannot play straight every time — cross-court shots can be effective — but if your opponent has not been drawn out of position first, the ball must be aimed to strike the side wall opposite where he is standing. This shot will then either stretch him to the side or force him to retreat and play the ball from further back in the court.

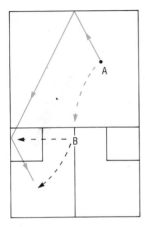

Figure 11 Your opponent has to do some very fast decision-making if you bounce the ball off the side wall exactly opposite his position.

Tactical summary

The importance of getting to the T and of playing straight cannot be emphasised too strongly. If you keep these objectives in mind and keep your eye on the ball, you will have the basis of a sound tactical approach.

Remember, the straight shot earns you the right to the T; after that it is simply a case of playing the ball *away* from your opponent — if he is at the back, play it short; if he is at the front, play it deep.

Simple, isn't it? The only snag is that your opponent is trying to do the same to you, so the battle for the T can become quite interesting!

8

The basic drives

It is no good going into battle with tactics but no weapons, so in this chapter we look at your armoury of strokes.

A good compact swing on both sides is an essential ingredient of the basic strokes. You should already have practised some "shadow" strokes to give you a feel of the racket.

Open and closed
If the racket face is inclined backwards when it hits the ball, it is said to be *open*. Not surprisingly, the opposite of this is referred to as being *closed*. If the racket face is closed, the ball is likely to go down.

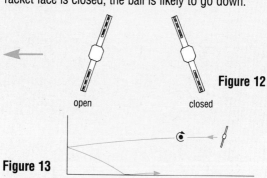

Figure 12

open   closed

Figure 13

The main use of an open face when making a stroke is to put a little backspin onto the ball when playing to the front wall. This makes the ball rebound down to the floor faster than hitting with the face perpendicular to the floor, and can often cause problems for your opponent.

The stroke is timed to meet the ball at the top of its bounce, so that the strings impart a "cut" as the ball contacts them.

The second use of the open face is to achieve height in strokes such as the serve and the lob.

Forehand drive

The first stroke to master is the forehand drive. There are three important stages of the basic stroke:

Stage 1: preparation
Jon is well balanced and ready to strike; he holds the racket head high, well back and slightly open (photo 15).

Stage 2: striking
He strikes the ball when it is a comfortable distance away, and level with his front knee (photo 16).

Stage 3: follow-through
The end of the follow-through: note how the racket head has followed the intended path of the ball and finished in a high position (photo 17). This will enable Jon to keep the racket up as he recovers to the T and prepares for his opponent's return.

15

16

17

Forehand drive clinic

Erratic direction
If you are having trouble with the direction of your shots, check the three *Bs* — *Bat*, *Body* and *Ball* — the positions of which are all inter-related.

If you have followed the instructions and developed a sound swing, then the *bat* should be OK; if you are arriving sideways to make the stroke, the *body* is correct; that leaves the *ball* as the likely source of your problem!

Figure 14 shows the ball when it is played from different positions relative to your leading leg.

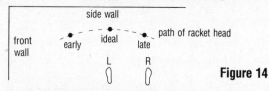

Figure 14

The central position is the ideal one for the straight forehand drive.

If you take the ball in front of your leading leg, it is said to have been taken *early*. This tends to make the ball go cross-court even though you are convinced that you aimed straight.

If you hit too late — after the ball has passed your leading leg — it will probably hit the side wall either on the way to the front wall or on its return journey. Either way the ball comes out into the court and presents an easier opportunity for your opponent.

Power
When attempting to hit the ball harder, many players rotate their shoulders as they strike. Sometimes the action is so pronounced that you can see their whole trunk twisting with each stroke. This is a *body* fault and usually results in an inability to hit straight. Make sure that all your power comes from the timing of your strike.

Swing
If you fail to keep the swing of the racket under control — for example by allowing your wrist to be loose — the ball can go anywhere. This is really a *bat* problem, but the *body* plays a part in it too. Although your opponent won't know where the ball is going, you won't either, so the advantage will be slight!

An uncontrolled swing can be dangerous: the rules allow a referee to penalise players who have an excessive swing.

Backhand drive

For most players the backhand drive is a more natural stroke than the forehand, but it demands particular care in positioning.

Stage 1: preparation
Clare takes up position for the backhand drive (photo 18). She is facing the left-hand wall and has the head of the racket high.

Stage 2: striking
The ball is struck when it is slightly *ahead* of her right leg (photo 19). This is very important.

Stage 3: follow-through
Clare's follow-through is smooth, and the racket head is kept high (photo 20).

18

19

20

Clare demonstrates the backhand drive. Note where the ball is relative to her foot when she hits it, and the high position of the racket head at the end of the stroke.

Backhand drive clinic

Just as when playing on the forehand, *bat*, *body* and *ball* are the elements which you have to get right.

The *bat* is easily taken care of by keeping your grip firm, and starting the stroke with the racket at a good height.

The *body* needs more careful consideration: positioning is the key to a good backhand drive. The secret is not to get too close to the ball.

21

In photo 21 Jon is so close that he has had to drop the racket head to make contact. His wrist has flopped, and his thumb is down the shaft as he pokes at the ball.

22

Plenty of errors in photo 22 too! Jon has "opened" his shoulders in an attempt to get at a close ball; he is also badly balanced and could strike Clare with the racket as his follow-through may be uncontrolled. Clare isn't doing very well either: her previous shot has not earned her the right to be there on the T, she's not watching her opponent, and her racket is hardly in a prepared position.

Getting in the right position relative to the *ball* is vital for a good backhand. Beginners often tend to be too far "ahead" of the ball to play it effectively. When you face a side wall ready to play a forehand stroke, your racket arm will be further away from the front wall than your body and consequently you have more space on this side. However, this changes when you line up to play a backhand stroke: your arm is now nearer to the front wall than your body. You must create the space by making sure that the ball is slightly ahead of your leading leg as you strike.

Producing pace
Although the backhand is a much more natural stroke than the forehand, many players get disastrous results when they strive for greater pace. Power on the backhand side comes from good rotation of the *body* during preparation, and accurate timing when striking the *ball*.

9

More strokes

A good grounding in the two basic drives will reap its rewards, because all the following strokes are modified versions of the basics.

Strokes fall into two categories:

● those you use by choice

● those you are forced to play.

The former are generally attacking shots and the others defensive, although if the latter are played well they can lead you into an attacking situation.

The serve

Remember, to satisfy the rules when serving, you must stand with at least one foot within the lines of the service box. Hit the ball so that it strikes the front wall between the cut line and the boundary line and then rebounds into the opposite back quarter of the court.

In a successful serve, the ball will strike the opposite side wall extremely close to the boundary line. Accuracy will come with regular practice. You are not under pressure when you serve, so there is no excuse for failing to develop a good service.

In the examples given below, both the players are right-handed: left-handed players should reverse the instructions.

Service from the right-hand box

Jon throws the ball up so that he is able to hit at a comfortable distance from his body (photo 23). Note that the racket face is "open" in order to project the ball upwards. He aims at a point roughly half-way across the front wall so that the ball will reach the opposite side wall above the rear of the left-hand serving box.

23 **24**

Service from the left-hand box

When serving from the left-hand box, Jon aims for a point to the right of centre on the front wall (photo 24). The ball will rebound through a relatively narrow angle to arrive above the back of the right-hand box. You can see that his racket is much nearer to the centre of the court when he serves from this side.

A good serve from the left calls for greater accuracy than one from the right. This is because the ball travels through a narrower angle, and a slight misjudgement will lead to a large error.

An accurate serve from either side will enable you to take up residence on the T and establish control from the outset. Remember to keep your eye on the ball and enjoy the fun in the back corner!

Return of serve

You won't succeed at squash unless you can develop a good return of serve.

The server has a distinct advantage: if the service is made well, it will go to the rear of the court. The server will therefore be in front of you and can easily take up a position on the T. Therefore the prime object of the service return is to remove that advantage.

Figure 15 shows one way this can be done. Any attempt to make a cross-court return will be playing into your opponent's hands: you can see that the shot to play is a straight, deep return which will force your opponent off the T and enable you to take his place.

In photo 24 Clare has taken up a good position for receiving Jon's serve — she is a stride away from the corner of the service box and her body faces along the diagonal of that box. Her racket is up, and she is watching the ball comfortably from her "open" stance — a common fault is to turn towards the side wall too early.

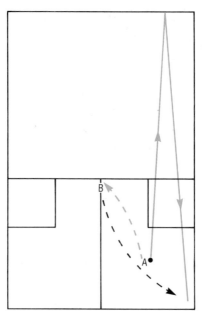

Figure 15 A straight down-the-wall return is often the best answer to a serve. By doing so, A has forced B into the rear corner, so that A can take his place on the T.

If Jon's serve is loose, Clare will have no trouble in moving into position to take full advantage of his error with a drive down the wall. If the serve is a good one, Clare has two choices:

● step forward to volley the ball

● leave it to rebound off the side wall and onto the floor, then try to solve the problem in the back corner (see "The boast", page 44).

Make the effort to develop a good serve and return of service. Rallies are short when you are starting in squash, and many points are won or lost in the first few strokes.

The volley

The volley is a stroke which is played *before* the ball bounces on the floor.

The volley uses more of a punching action than the drives, as the backswing and follow-through are shorter: all the other basic ingredients are similar. Always strike with a firm wrist, and don't be concerned that there is no time to take a full swing.

The key factors in playing a volley are:

- keep your eye on the ball
- keep your racket up
- quick anticipation.

Clare "punches" a forehand volley.

Tactically it makes good sense to volley whenever the chance arises. As mentioned in the previous section, it can be a useful way of returning serve, and can also be used at other times in a rally to prevent you from being driven into the back corners.

Most volleys are played from around the T area, and good volleying will allow you to retain dominance in that position. The volley speeds up the game and forces your opponent to hurry between shots, so is an important weapon to have in your armoury.

Volley clinic

- Accuracy is more important than pace: beginners often try to hit their volleys too hard.

- Failing to get your shoulders round to face the side wall is as common a problem in volleying as when playing the drives.

Volley practice
A simple method of building up confidence in your technique is to hit a series of continuous volleys to yourself. Start by standing fairly close to the wall and hit the ball against it at a comfortable height. As success breeds confidence, move further back until ultimately you can play the ball repeatedly from around the short line to the front wall.

The boast

The boast is really a drive which is deliberately played onto the side wall of the court. Depending on which side of the court you are, it will be either a forehand or a backhand shot. You strike the ball as if you were going to knock it through the wall into the opposite front corner of the next-door court.

Figure 16 shows the path the ball will take when a forehand boast is played: the geometry of the squash court is such that the ball will eventually arrive in the backhand front corner. If you fix this path firmly in your mind, you will soon be able to use the boast successfully.

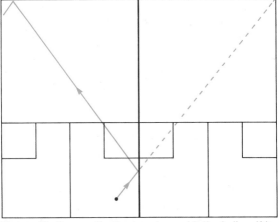

Figure 16 For an effective boast, you hit the ball as if it is going to travel through the wall to the far corner of the next court!

When to use the boast

Inevitably there will be times when your opponent gains the upper hand and you have to do the work! You will find that it is sometimes impossible to play straight if you are forced deep into the court with the ball going past you. This is when your early enemy, the side wall, becomes your ally: by deliberately striking the ball towards the side wall you can make it reach the front wall in the opposite front corner. Played in this way, the boast is a defensive shot, and this is its chief value to you as a beginner. Concentrate on using it to get out of difficult situations. A typical case arises when the ball is at the rear of the court.

Figure 17 shows a movement pattern which creates space for you to hit the ball *at* the forehand side wall.

If the boast is played by choice during an exchange down the side wall, it can also become a useful attacking weapon.

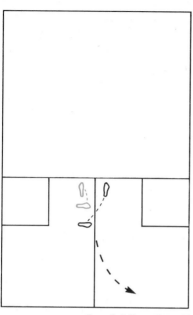

Figure 17
Creating space to play a boast — remember, turn first, then move.

Boast follow-through

As the stroke is played close to the wall, you need to modify your follow-through. Take your racket upwards after the strike, so that you do not add to the "wear and tear" marks in the corner.

Boast clinic

The majority of beginners make one of two errors:

● to use too much power, which usually results in the racket face becoming "closed" and the ball going down.

● to rotate the body, particularly the shoulders, in an attempt to *help* the ball to the front — this technique results in the ball skidding along the side wall and coming out into mid-court where the opponent gleefully accepts it.

The secret is to get the direction right first, and then to open the face of the racket so that you hit the ball upwards onto the side wall. You may need to get down to the shot by bending your knees. If you get the initial flight of the ball right, from racket to wall, the rest will look after itself!

Photos 26 and 27 show the preparation and strike position of Jon's forehand boast, while 28 and 29 show Clare's backhand boast.

Compared with the forehand, remember to make more space on the backhand, as your racket arm will be closer to the wall.

29   28

The lob

The lob is a "finesse" shot which is played with delicate control. It is used primarily for defence, but can also be a very useful means of attack. It is most commonly played from the front of the court: the ball is hit upwards against the front wall so that it rebounds well over the head of your opponent, who will almost certainly be standing at the T. In this defensive guise, a lob buys you time, as he has to wait for the ball to come down.

Lob technique

The lob is normally played with a very open racket face. The whole point is for the ball to have plenty of height as it travels back across the court.

In photos 30 and 31, both Jon and Clare are hitting *early* relative to their bodies. The ball will go across the court towards the opposite back corner. Note how the racket face is very open in both cases.

With practice you can perfect the lob so that the ball "dies" in the back corners. This makes it a powerful attacking weapon.

Left: the forehand lob —
Jon bends low and
opens the face of the
racket.

Below: the backhand lob
— Clare takes the ball
well in front of her leading leg.

31

The drop shot

The perfect drop is a short, low shot which, after con-
tacting the front wall, "dies" in the *nick*, as the junction
between the side walls and the floor is called.

Jon and Clare demonstrate the drop shot in photos
32 and 33. They are both well balanced and in a good
position to recover after the shot by pushing off on the
leading leg.

If your previous shot has forced your opponent to
boast from a back corner, following it up with a drop
shot can be devastating. He now has to travel from the
back corner to the opposite front corner where you have
played your drop shot — this is the longest journey on
a squash court. As well as being rather satisfying, being
able to send your opponent all over the court like this
shows that you are acquiring good tactical skills.

Above: *the forehand drop — Jon is well-balanced, and strikes the ball at the top of the bounce.*

Right: *the backhand drop; Clare looks very comfortable as she guides the ball towards the nick.*

33

Far too often players will stand to admire the drop shot they have just played and then cannot get to the next ball when their opponent surprises them. Even though your drop shot may look like a winner, you must always assume that your opponent will get to it: position yourself in readiness to take advantage of what will surely be a weak return — don't throw away your good work by being over-confident.

Drop shot clinic
Many players, even experienced ones, make the mistake of aiming the ball too low in their search for perfection. This often results in an embarrassing contact with the tin. It is better to play a "working" drop, which hits the front wall and then a side wall *before* the floor.

10

Practices

There's a well-known story about Gary Player, the famous South African golfer, which always comes to mind when discussing practice. His ball was in a bunker by the eighteenth green, and he needed to hole it in two strokes to force a play-off in a championship. Player chipped straight into the hole to win outright, and somewhere in the crowd a voice called "You lucky so-and-so, Player", to which he replied "Y'know, it's funny, the more I practise, the luckier I get."

Practice is important in any sport, and even the simplest practice requires the vital qualities of concentration and discipline. Fortunately there is such a variety of practices in squash that it need never become boring.

There are three groups of practices:

● ball-sense practices

● solo practices

● pairs routines, both co-operative and competitive.

The routines and exercises which follow are for beginners in squash: they provide a good introduction to the type of work which will help you to improve your game. As you progress, you will use many other routines to develop both fitness and skill.

Ball-sense practices

Before starting, always ensure that your grip is correct — check this frequently in the early days.

1 Place the ball on the forehand face of the racket and bounce it off the strings into the air repeatedly. Count the bounces. If you score more than fifty consecutively, move on; less than fifty — keep practising!

2 Repeat the bouncing exercise on the backhand face, but *do not* change the grip.

3 Repeat the bouncing exercise, but using alternate faces of the racket: note that you do not have time to change the grip!

You can do the previous exercises anywhere, but you need to be on a squash court for the rest:

4 Play a continuous rally against the wall, using your forehand: *hit, wall, bounce, hit, wall, bounce.* Pay attention to style: turn sideways, keep the racket head above your wrist, and bend your knees when necessary. Keep a count of the number of successive shots. You can vary your distance from the wall as your confidence and ability improve.

34

Playing a continuous rally on the forehand. Practise keeping the sideways position, with bent knees and good balance.

5 Repeat exercise 4, but on your backhand — remember not to change your grip.

6 Now repeat the exercise, alternating forehand and backhand. This needs speedy footwork, and you must not cheat by simply facing the wall.

7 Volley practice: repeat exercises 4, 5 and 6 but without allowing the ball to bounce.

Keep practising these ball-sense exercises until you can reach a score of fifty on all of them. Of course, you can try other practices before reaching this standard, but do keep going back to improve your score — and your confidence!

Solo stroke practices

In this series of exercises you "feed" the ball to yourself. That in itself can be an art, but remember, "the more you practise, the luckier you get". The instructions are given for right-handed players; left-handers should reverse right and left.

Forehand drive

● Face the wall with your left foot on the short line about half-way between the T and the service box, with your racket held in readiness for the stroke.

● Throw the ball from your left hand, either straight up into the air or via the side wall. It should bounce to "sit up" in front of your left leg so that you can strike it comfortably.

● Play the ball to the front wall, concentrating on accuracy and style.

You may require a few attempts to get the co-ordination of the feed correct, particularly as you are throwing left-handed. You will soon discover how much height is needed to give the ball a big enough bounce.

If you are rebounding the ball from the wall, a common fault is to throw too hard so that it comes back too close to your body.

Do not, at this stage, attempt to play continuous shots. Pick up the ball between shots and concentrate on good preparation. Try to keep all your shots parallel to the side wall.

As you get the feel of it, set yourself targets: try to hit six successive perfect forehands, then increase this to ten. Soon you will be able to aim for different lengths, perhaps making the ball bounce behind the short line, then behind the service box.

Finally, progress to a continuous rally, introducing tighter targets and striving for higher numbers of perfect repetitions. Don't forget the importance of good technique: if things go wrong, especially if it is a consistent fault, use the *bat/body/ball* checklist for self-diagnosis (see page 36).

Backhand drive

● You can practise the backhand drive in virtually the same way as the forehand. It will probably take a few tries before you get the feed right.

● When you strike, it is very important that you are further from the front wall than the ball is.

Clare sets up for a backhand drive — it is important to throw the ball to the right of your leading leg.

- When you graduate to playing continuous backhand practice rallies, it becomes absolutely essential for the ball *always* to be nearer to the front wall than your body is.

Volleys

- Improve volleying by using an extension of ball-sense practice 7 (see page 50): this time, gradually move further away from the front wall towards the short line. Keep the rally going for as long as possible.

- One of the best ways to practise volleying is to incorporate volleys into rally routines close to both the side walls. This mixture of strokes will add extra movement and change of pace into the rallies.

The boast
The boast can be one of the most rewarding strokes for solo practice.

- To practise the boast, use a hand feed to the side wall from a position behind the service box.

- Hit the ball as described on page 44 — imagine that you are trying to hit it through the wall into the opposite front corner of the next-door court. When you get the flight and angles right, the ball will hit three walls — side, front and opposite side — and eventually roll back across the floor to where you are standing.

Have another look at photos 26 and 28 (page 46) to set up your initial position.

● Practise both forehand and backhand boasts.

● The ultimate ego trip is to practise the boast as a return to your own serve — if you cannot make the boast it is because of the quality of your serve, but if your boast reaches the front wall correctly you can pat yourself on the back for that!

Solo practices are a great way of improving your anticipation, movement and balance. Don't cheat though — to be of any value, all these practices must be performed properly!

Practice in pairs

Practice is a lot more fun if you have a partner on court. You should start with co-operative work and then progress to competitive practice. In the early stages it is best for one player to feed the ball by hand. Here are some ideas:

Forehand drive
The feeder throws the ball from a position on the short line to hit the front wall near the cut line. The partner starts on the T and moves forward to play the ball. If there are problems at first, try moving nearer to the front wall, gain confidence and then gradually move further back.

36

In photo 36, Jon feeds so that Clare can move in to play a forehand drive.

Once this is going smoothly, try feeding with the racket instead of hand feeding. Progress to setting targets: you will soon be confident enough to try a co-operative rally.

First rallies

At first, stand one on each side of the court, and hit the ball backwards and forwards via the front wall. The object is to keep the rally going, not to beat your opponent, so count the number of shots in the rally and then aim to increase the score.

You will soon be able to introduce variations to make the practice more interesting. Try changing sides, and perhaps setting higher standards such as "no backhand strokes allowed on the forehand side", or "all shots must hit the front wall below the cut line".

Rallies down the side walls

Your first attempt at a rally down the side wall must be well organised. This routine works well:

Player A stands behind the service box and feeds from the racket. Player B operates from the T, returning there after each shot. Play starts with A feeding a short ball to the front wall so that B has to move from the T and play a deep drive before returning. Player A then feeds short again, and the practice continues.

Start by feeding single shots and progress to continuous feeding as your skills improve. The next stage is for each player to move to the T after his shot, with A still playing from the back and B from the front.

Safety note

By keeping to a set movement pattern at this stage you will be avoiding dangerous situations while you develop your skill. Always be prepared to stop if you feel that your racket or the ball may hit your partner. You will need to keep this rule in mind as you move on to the next stage, in which play will be much more vigorous. Remember that you are still co-operating, so do your best to get out of each other's way after playing a shot, and only return to the T *if it is safe to do so*.

Drive rallies

It can be very satisfying to get a good rally going in which both players aim to hit the ball beyond the short line. This is when you begin to learn the way to move around each other. Some players get the idea that there are set rules for movement patterns, such as "clockwise on the left of the court and anticlockwise on the right", but this is not the case. The rule-book simply states that you must do your utmost to give your opponent access to the ball — if you do not, you will be penalised. How you move is up to you!

Care taken during these early co-operative rallies will create good habits for the hurly-burly of competition later.

Competitive practices for pairs

Most of the co-operative practices can be made competitive by introducing targets and scores. For example, in the forehand-drive exercise, you can score a point every time your drive lands over the short line. Play to twenty feeds, then change places.

The alley game

Practices which concentrate on accuracy alone can be quite satisfying, but for most players the real fun starts when you try to play shots which would defeat an opponent. For example, during a rally down the side wall, you can try to place the ball so that it cannot be returned down the same side wall.

This is popularly known as the "alley game". The "court" is defined as an extension of the service box to the front and back, rather similar to the tramlines on a tennis doubles court. You both have to keep the ball within this narrow area as you play alternate strokes — a very effective way of practising your straight drives.

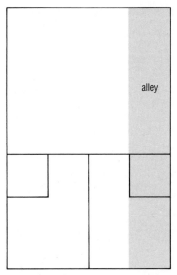

alley

Figure 18 The alley game. It looks simple, but you will be surprised how much concentration is needed to keep the ball within the narrow alley.

Combination contests

Strokes can be paired together in competition. Virtually any shots can be used, but a classic combination is *drive and boast*.

Player *A* starts with a forehand drive which *B* has to boast. The ball goes to *A*'s backhand side, where it is driven down the opposite wall so that *B*'s return has to be a backhand boast. A point is scored for every rally; as *A* has more chance of hitting winners with drives, he is likely to win, say, by 9–4. Then the players change places and *B* attempts to beat *A* by a wider margin.

Serve versus return is another popular combination. You can score in the same way as for *drive and boast*, or you can require the rally to be completed in a set number of shots, otherwise neither player scores. The possible combinations and scoring systems are endless and you will soon be making up your own to suit the circumstances.

It is true that your game will improve simply by playing a variety of opponents, but it will improve much more rapidly if you devote some time to practice. Some people find solo practice boring, but the drive and determination required to do it are qualities to be found in most successful players.

11

Rules clinic

The rules of the game are the responsibility of the International Squash Rackets Federation (ISRF), which was formed in 1967. From time to time — usually at four-year intervals — alterations are discussed and agreed upon at the Federation's AGM.

Although the printed *Rules of Squash Rackets*, which you can easily obtain from the Squash Rackets Association, appear long and complicated, many of them are really only of great concern when you get into serious competition. Provided that you play safely and respect the court-marking lines, you will not go far wrong to start with!

Problem questions

Here are some typical questions which newcomers to the game tend to ask:

Q *If I serve from the wrong service box, do I lose the rally?*
A No. If your opponent makes no attempt to play the ball, the service is simply taken again, from the correct box. If the opponent does play the ball, it is just treated as a normal service.

Q *Can I bounce the ball before hitting it when serving?*
A No. You have to hit it directly from your hand, and it must travel straight to the front wall.

Q *If I lob the ball and it obviously goes above the out-of-court line before hitting a wall correctly, do I lose the point?*
A No. It is out only if it actually touches the wall above the line, or hits anything such as the ceiling, beams or lights.

Q *Is it OK to rebound the ball from the rear wall?*
A Yes. If you have the skill, there is nothing to stop you from using the back wall in just the same way as the others.

Q *Why do you spin a racket to settle who serves first — why not use a coin?*

A The *Rules of Squash* specify the spin of a racket.

Q *Why does a player who is obstructed sometimes get the rally awarded to him (a stroke), but at other times it is played again (a let)?*

A It all depends on the circumstances: *let* is the term used for an undecided rally; if you accidentally impede your opponent when he is not in a position to play a winner, but would otherwise have been able to make a good return, it is only fair to play the rally again. However, if your opponent was obviously in a position to play a winner when you impeded him, it is unfair to start again, and so he is awarded a *stroke*; i.e., he wins the rally.

Q *If the ball bounces awkwardly from something such as the door latch or broken plaster, is a let played?*

A No. Fittings or irregularities are treated as part of the court, and play continues normally.

Q *Can I insist that my opponent gets on with the next game without a pause?*

A No. The *Rules* allow an interval of 90 seconds between games.

Q *If my opponent hits me with the ball, does he win the point?*

A Not necessarily. If you get in the direct path of the ball on its way to the front wall, then he does win — usually. However, if his shot was definitely not going to be a good return, he loses.

Q *I got out of the way of the shot I expected from him, but the ball still hit me and he claimed the point; surely that wasn't fair?*

and

Q *I tried as hard as possible to give the other player access to the ball, but he still claimed a let. What more could I have done?*

A It is almost impossible to give a fair ruling on questions of obstruction and lets unless you have seen the incident. The best advice for beginners is always to play a let rather than risk injury. You can worry about the finer points when you have more experience of the game and are beginning to take a serious interest in match play.

Photo 38 shows the striker, Jansher Khan, impeded by his opponent Ross Norman, and to most observers this appears to be a case for a stroke to be awarded; however, we do not know how the incident arose. It may be that Ross Norman is having to take evasive action because the striker changed his mind about when to play his shot.

It will pay you to obtain an up-to-date set of the *Rules of Squash Rackets* and become familiar with them. You will be surprised at the misunderstandings many quite experienced players have. Also, beware of being taken in by "local rules" which players may claim — it is amazing how often these crop up!

Keeping score

When you are playing in friendly matches, you normally keep score informally as you go along. In more serious competitions there will be two officials to take care of this: a *marker* and a *referee*. The referee is the final authority in all matters of procedure and discipline on court. He can overrule the call of a marker, but would only do so if an obvious injustice or error seemed likely to pass uncorrected.

If you get the opportunity to attend a lecture for markers and referees, do go along and learn more about the rules — you cannot attend these sessions too often if you wish to gain a thorough understanding.

Gordon Freakes and author Barry Mason, marker and **39** *referee respectively, keep a critical eye on Chris Robertson as he plays a delicate backhand drop.*

12

How the sport is run

Squash is administered world-wide by the International Squash Rackets Federation (ISRF) and the game is governed in each affiliated country by its own national association.

In England, until recently, there were two separate associations for men and women: the Squash Rackets Association (SRA) and the Women's Squash Rackets Association (WSRA). They amalgamated in September 1989 after a long period during which the two associations worked together in specific areas such as coaching and refereeing. In Ireland there are still two separate associations; in Scotland and Wales the associations have always included both women and men.

The SRA National Coaches Committee monitors the award of coaching qualifications, and the Squash Referees Society does likewise for the qualification of officials.

Most of the other squash-playing countries operate a similar administration structure. Often the national body is staffed by paid officials, while affairs at county or regional level are taken care of by volunteer officials who devote much of their time to the development of squash purely for love of the sport.

Competition structure

One of the best ways to improve your squash is by competing with players who can stretch your abilities. Most clubs operate a league system which provides active competition for the members, and there are plenty of inter-club competitions. If you get a bit more serious, you can set your feet on the rungs of the competition ladder which reaches from club-level sport right up to the British Open Championship and its counterparts in other countries.

At junior level, promising players graduate from club to county squads and from there may be selected for their area squad, with the ultimate goal being a place in the national team.

Inter-county team competitions are organised nationally in a wide variety of categories, from under-16s to over-55s (the vintage class).

Around the world there is a similar range of competitions. Top tournaments for the leading professional players are co-ordinated in a world-wide circuit. The interests of these players are catered for by the International Squash Players Association (ISPA), which administers a world ranking list.

Useful addresses

British Isles

Squash Rackets Association
WestPoint
33–34 Warple Way
Acton
London
W3 0RQ

Irish Squash Rackets Association &
Irish Women's Squash Rackets Association
House of Sport
Long Mile Road
Dublin 12
Ireland

Scottish Squash Rackets Association
Caledonia House
South Gyle
Edinburgh
EH12 9DQ

Welsh Squash Rackets Federation
7 Kyman Terrace
Penarth
South Glamorgan
CF6 1AP

Overseas

Australian Squash Rackets Association
PO Box 356
Spring Hill
Queensland 4004
Australia

Canadian Squash Rackets Association
333 River Road
Ottawa
Ontario
K1L 8H9
Canada

The Squash Rackets Federation of India
c/o The Calcutta Racket Club
Nr St Paul's Cathedral
Chowringhee
Calcutta 700071
India

New Zealand Squash Rackets Association
PO Box 1040
Tauranga
New Zealand

Pakistan Squash Rackets Federation
Rear Air Headquarters
Peshawar
Cantt
Pakistan

United States Squash Rackets Association Inc
211 Ford Road
Bala-Cynwyd
PA 19004
USA

International

International Squash Rackets Federation
93 Cathedral Road
Cardiff
CF1 9PG
United Kingdom